From Preschool to the Penitentiary

A Candid Examination of a

Vicious Cycle

Duane Campbell

African American

IMAGES

Chicago, Illinois

Front cover illustration by Damon Stanford

First Edition, First Printing

Printed in the United States of America

ISBN #: 0-910030-14-6

ISBN #: 978-0910030144

Dedication

This body of work and all else that I do, is dedicated to that awesome power which is often silent, but forever quaking to shake into consciousness, the oftentimes sleeping souls of men.

To that one whose light shines so brilliantly that it dares to crack the cloak of our darkness—but is not blinding to our inner eye.

To the seed which manifests itself to give birth to the genius, within which I cannot explain, nor can I comprehend.

You are the power within, though somehow beyond myself; you have granted me the vision and the reality to know that all things are truly possible.

Duane Campbell

The Awareness Project

Contents

Systematic Factors

What Is The Awareness Project?

Conditions

Outreach: Intangibles

Introduction

From Preschool to the Penitentiary is an in-depth examination of a decimating cycle that tests the fragile balances of power and privilege, leaving an entire culture in search of an "American Dream" draped in misconception. Most of young black people's lives are spent in utter confusion, hopelessness and rage as they strive to achieve a direction of positive mobility—and all the while, they listen to the critics who state that they are nothing more than a "lost" and "wasted" generation.

Many poor and minority youth are used as statistical funding sources for various law enforcement strategies. Tested in many communities for feasibility and rationale, the strategies and initiatives focus on populations involved in legalized drug dealing and the rapidly growing industrialized prison complex. The populations under study are seen as mentally inferior and incapable of coexisting within the so-called "common flow" of society. Ultimately, many of them are economically coaxed into the American military machine to defend a social system that is oppressing their social, economic and psychological development.

Our youth culture, growing more rebellious and intolerant of these debilitating ideologies and policies are turning to alternative strategies of survival, such as: gangs, drugs, pimping, prostitution, and other avenues of violent and counterproductive behaviors.

The realities that we as community leaders, parents, teachers, clergy, law enforcement, youth, and youth-focused professionals are confronted with are indeed dire and present a

Introduction

formidable challenge to assure the positive direction of our society.

Confronting and engaging the many conditions which perpetuate our dilemma is vital to examining the underlying causes and effects responsible in the creation and maintenance of this vicious cycle which not only plagues our youth, but jeopardizes the whole of our society.

Also under discussion is the hypocrisy of the older generation, as it appears more evident that we have relinquished our responsibilities to assist in the social and moral transcendence of our youth and their culture. Our irresponsible tendency is complicated by a diminishing communicational relationship that is immensely vital in our efforts to reach out and relate to them as they search for constructive guidance.

As a culture and a nation are we willing to make the necessary commitment and sacrifices essential to correcting the course of this vicious cycle of destructive development? Are we willing to compel a change in the preschool-to-penitentiary ideology that America seems intent on implementing among poor and minority youth, or shall the rhetoric of American justice remain as a testament to one of our greatest hypocrisies?

This work focuses on a totality of inequality and injustice, born from the systematic processes of a society gone awry, entrenched ideologically into the American social structure. Lost within the greatness of its own rhetoric, America has created at the opposite end of the social elite a counter-society (if you will), consisting of social, moral and psychological depravation.

From Pre-School to the Penitentiary:
A Candid Examination of a Vicious Cycle

From the perspective of our children—many of whom are lost within the nation's educational and criminal justice systems—who live and toil in abject poverty and drug-infested communities, there is a hierarchy of their demise. As any people want to do, our youth try to make sense of what is happening to them, their culture and their surroundings as they construct and navigate the systematic philosophies of an unjust and socially biased system of mobility.

After an overview of the crisis facing poor and minority youth, this book looks at five trends that poor, black and brown youth routinely contend with at present:

- Criminal Justice/Injustice

- The Educational System

- The Community

- Family Structure and History

- The American Dream

The Appendix offers statistical follow-up for those who seek those types of details.

This book speaks boldly to our nation's top echelons of hierarchy. It speaks just as boldly to the misdirected power bases within these communities of social depravation. The church, the family, the youth, community leaders and adults' compromised ideologies are among the groups and individuals to whom youth look for appropriate, firm, clear, and ethical guidance—and all too often we fail them in this regard.

Introduction

The challenges before us are daunting.

The evolution of our actions as they relate to the development of our youth and the downtrodden of our society has produced devastating and long lasting effects, resulting from a perpetual conditioning process of social and moral depravation.

To transcend the conditional realities of this vicious and unrelenting cycle, we must endeavor to objectively confront the true essence of our own spiritual and moral character. Our entire culture dwells within the hypocrisies of a structural ideology born from an oppressive system that either consciously or unconsciously remains suppressive in its production.

My personal reckoning with the urgency and multi-layered facets of this developmental need for betterment led me to conceive and establish The Awareness Project. Details of this project are introduced in part here as a way to promote in-depth solutions for the whole of society.

After discovering some basic information about The Awareness Project, the reader can then learn more about community empowerment—a condition by which true progress can happen—and move on to pinpoint four intangibles for undertaking authentic outreach among youth. If we as adults are to engage in concrete improvement of the trends our youth face, we must pursue some fundamental ways in which we work toward helping and empowering them, including:

- Atmospheric (the environmental conditions in which youth live)

From Pre-School to the Penitentiary:
A Candid Examination of a Vicious Cycle

- Inner Development/Self-Realization (the priority we give to the spiritual, emotional and psychological development of ourselves and our youth)

- Leadership (the kinds of leadership structures and styles embedded in American culture and the issues about leadership blacks face as individuals and as a culture)

- Accountability (the means by which we bring follow-up to bear as we define ourselves and others)

The Summary wraps up the book's key issues and the Appendix features some facts that further illuminate the five Trends.

Ultimately, we must aggressively engage the injustices of a nation entrenched within its own misconceptions of racial, social and class definition that remain prevalent and infectious within our culture. We must reach out to one another and to our youth.

More and more, black youth are falling through the cracks of American justice, leading the nation proportionately in illiteracy, unjust law enforcement policies and brutality against black children. By proportion, blacks have the highest infant mortality rate in America, the highest poverty rate in America, and the highest incarceration rate in America, as our communities lay ravaged by the drug culture and black-on-black genocide.

The American sociological system is either hopelessly broken or drastically corrupted, from its most basic to its most complex levels. By either standard, something must be done to correct the course by which our new history is being etched. Our current reaction to these devastating circumstances of racial, social and psychological suppression exists as our most immediate burden to bear.

What follows is a bold and often scathing developmental concept, confronting real life issues that as a culture we appear to possess neither the will nor the skill to solve.

From Preschool to the Penitentiary is a candid examination of not only our youth and our culture, but of the essence of ourselves. As so-called mentors and leaders, we continue to turn a deaf ear to the intense rage and desperate cries of our children. If we are to continue the legacy of previous generations—including those who survived numerous challenges and broke barriers that failed to stymie their achievements—we must lead the way in "facing the rising sun...[as] we march on 'til victory is-won."[1]

Overview

The Crisis

If we would dare to take a candid and realistic look into the current developmental status of our youth culture in today's America, we would find a youth population faced not only with the systematic and societal "pull yourself up by your own bootstraps" pressures of status and achievement. More importantly, they're confronted with the psychological, emotional and moral breakdowns within our society that lead to heavy drug use, youth suicide, youth incarceration, gang life mentalities, an epidemic of infant mortality, youth homicide, and a self-fulfilling ideology of hopelessness which stunt the potential and smother the realm of possibilities within the youth psyche.

I am not at all stating that our youth population lacks achievement and greatness. But it would be a drastic mistake for people to use the mentality of "the cup is half full" when speaking of our most cherished and precious asset.

Among the most crippling and detrimental elements in relation to the positive development of our youth are the lack of positive leadership and the sheer abandonment of our youth by the older adult population. In many of my lectures and seminars, I often candidly address the issue of how the older adult generation has in essence compromised or "sold out" our youth, relinquishing any culpability relating to the reality of their current condition.

Overview

If one were to ponder why increasingly more of our youth population has stepped farther and farther outside the footsteps of their predecessors, one would find that the

most basic levels of admiration and respect have all but vanished within the perceptions and ideology of youth and adult relationships.

We as adults and mentors of our youth's generation have drastically failed them in our instances of outreach related to our development, commitment and support.

Our youth are manifesting the rage of a generation. The adversarial conditions of hopelessness, psychological oppression and spiritual depravation are directly affecting the entire youth culture; primarily affected are the black, brown and poorer youth populations in America.

We as a society must now seek out new avenues to create and implement innovative concepts and strategies designed to address and uplift a youth culture in crisis.

For too long we have avoided going deeply into the causes and effects of this counterproductive spiral which has stunted the growth and development of a truly great and powerful generation. Instead, we have polluted the development and perceptions of youths' self-images with the faces and actions of weak leadership—hypocritical social and spiritual icons and counterproductive role models.

What we have denied our youth runs far deeper than a part-time job or the empty promise of a better tomorrow.

From Pre-School to the Penitentiary:
A Candid Examination of a Vicious Cycle

Something is missing within the cultural development of our youth that money cannot buy.

Many of the structural concepts of youth outreach and development must be reevaluated and eventually restructured to adapt to the realities of their dilemma, as they relate to the broader perceptions of cause and effect that lay the foundation and perpetuate further this vicious cycle of counterproduction.

There are many social and psychological elements that serve to create and sustain the momentum of this cycle. Many of these elements can be attributed to the neglectful and socially compromising mind-set of the adult population, the church's lost outreach and embrace, the racist and class biased hierarchy of American justice, and the unequal and inept outreach of the educational system. Our inability or unwillingness to confront ourselves without the veils of hypocrisy and arrogant self-perception has been the catalyst perpetuating this vicious and unrelenting cycle of spiritual, social and psychological depravation deeply infecting the developmental consciousness and moral character of our youth and our culture.

The proportions of black and brown youth demonstrate the realities of poverty and neglect that far exceeds that of their white counterparts. The so-called masterminds of American political and social strategies, create and enact legislation designed to keep under subjugation the poor and uninitiated of our society. All this and more speaks to the hypocrisy of a nation that mimics the ideology of its own creed.

Overview

The overall apathy of American society existing in our time dictates a repetitive cycle of social, moral and psychological repression that has in essence created the disenfranchisement of an entire race and culture. Mobility today is greatly compromised, resulting in the evolution of a calculating, brutal and oppressive social and human condition that has the great potential to modify individual and societal character.

We have come to a culturally destructive crossroads, where we find an entire generation buying into the painful reality that they are in all actuality left to find their own avenues of fulfillment and character. Our youth must serve as their own caretakers—they must "grow themselves" up solely by their own independent perceptions of self-analysis and discovery.

The crisis among youth plagues all of America, ultimately threatening the future development of our society. This crisis is a culmination of events, manifested throughout the course of our racist, class-defined and oppressive history. As such, this crisis involves a cycle which threatens all who, despite oppressive social and psychological conditioning, have adapted to survive within the mental and physical terrain of their environments.

Cycles either spin infinitum, or until they are no more, or they are influenced by some event—redirected in their definition and direction to alter the course of their development. America is in transition.

Our resistance to embracing compassion, our inability or unwillingness to uplift the least of us within our society, our arrogance to insist that we are a nation of just and unbiased laws, and our hypocrisy to speak of the "American Dream" that has been realized by the infliction of a nightmare upon others brings into question the direction and ultimate fate of American society.

The crisis confronting our children was not created by their own design, but by ours—the past and current caretakers of the American condition.

While this crisis plagues all of America and most critically its children, the heaviest of the burden falls on black, brown and poor children in this country, skewing their visions of a productive future while condemning them to the prisons and ghettos of America and a broken and biased educational system.

The arrogance and hypocrisy of America's elite levels of hierarchy states that the playing field of mobility has been leveled and made plain upon the American landscape of productive possibilities, as though the course of time has healed our wounds. These current conditions exist, discounting the long lasting effects of the cycle, manifested by the initial implementation of the condition itself. From the advent of the African slave trade to present-day America, the vestiges of oppression exist, inferiority and injustice that have been etched into the psyche and innate thought processes of black people in America and throughout the world.

There are those who do not possess, or even seek to possess the understanding of how the processes of social, spiritual and psychological conditioning can exist within a generational context. The process of osmosis as it relates to the social and psychological conditioning of a culture is used to instill a seemingly permanent sense of self-inferiority. This process also reinforces perpetually the self-maintenance of a deeply rooted sense of unworthiness and the negative emotion of a conflicting inner struggle that unbalances the developmental cycle of the oppressed and uninitiated.

This crisis speaks to the evolution of a culture, currently hanging in the balance and bogged down between rebellion and repetition. However, the dynamics of life—even life as stunted as is often the case among today's poor and minority youth—demands that we search for a new ideology to redefine our participation, that we reconstruct the broken dream and broken promise that is America.

Those who state that this legacy is not of their own design, but instead belongs to those who came before them; who state that the long lasting vestiges of oppression, discrimination and racism indelibly etched within the psyche of our culture are nothing more than the residue of a lost and misled idea, fail to comprehend the very real effects upon the social, spiritual and psychological development of a specific race or culture and their young people. Just as we must recognize the effect or else doom another generation to the kind of life experiences prevalent today, we also must realize there are paths ahead which can signal real progress—and we can take responsibility for creating and implementing these paths.

We must remain diligent and forever mindful of the innate thought processes of a culture in rebellion; born of their separation from their inner self and ready access to the developmental mind-set of their own greatness. As it stands now, our children are left to somehow fend for themselves on the battlefield of the American Dream. This is unacceptable.

From Pre-School to the Penitentiary:
A Candid Examination of a Vicious Cycle

It has been said, "The arc of the moral universe is long, but bends toward justice."[2] It is our hope that morality is within America's social, spiritual and ideological character.

With seemingly no support or embrace from the upper echelons of America or their predecessors before them, black children and ultimately all children in America are in a very realistic sense within a crisis not of their making. Surely, one of their challenges and ours is to overcome it.

Trends

Criminal Justice/Injustice

The term "criminal justice/injustice" is not a play on words as much as it is a play on the implementation of American social ideology and policy. The scales of justice in America remain so diametrically opposed that there no longer exists even an effort of deception attempted to skew its reality.

The main burden bearer of the criminal justice/injustice system was, is, and will remain the black male in America. Few would debate this statement given the disproportionate numbers of black males indicted and incarcerated in the U.S.[3] What many fail to realize or to acknowledge, however, are the devastating and long lasting effects pertaining to incarceration, or the conditions resulting from entrapment within the system itself; i.e., probation, parole, felony conviction. These conditions essentially separate the black male from his family and community, ultimately stunting and stagnating the developmental mind-set that is crucial to mental, spiritual and social growth of not only the victimized individual, but of an entire culture.

On many of the streets across America's inner cities, the criminal justice/injustice system's "protect and serve" mantra is no more than a sarcastic slogan used to project an atmosphere of public service and security. Throughout our history, however, the American design and implementation of racist, class-defined laws and violent acts of suppression, such as: the "Black Codes," the terrorist crusades of the Ku Klux Klan, the unjust "separate but equal" policies used in education, housing, voting rights, and jury nullification. Countless other basic human rights have stood as the standard-bearer of the racist and oppressive "status quo" of each era in which they have been featured as a daily part of life—some of which have recently been re-enacted.

Social and economic suppression within the communities of predominately black and brown America serves as an ironic prerequisite of entry into the industrialized criminal justice/injustice entity. The playing field of mobility as it exists in the poverty belt of America's inner cities is a counterproductive design of perpetual cause and effect, feeding the machine of the larger industrialized complex.

From a socioeconomic perspective, these industrialized complexes, utilized to warehouse the perceived "law breakers" of our land, also aid in sustaining the economies of many towns and cities throughout America.

The incentive to maintain a certain human capacity within these complexes greatly compromises the ethical and moral standards of law enforcement.

A vast majority of black and brown America dwells within the social and economic underclass of American society, as the existence of poverty, complicated by the educational chasm, has proven to be an historical constant in America, separating upward mobility between the upper and lower classes of American society. The economically challenged black and brown segments of our society; many of whom are male, serve as feeders into the mechanisms of the criminal justice/injustice system.

From Pre-School to the Penitentiary:
A Candid Examination of a Vicious Cycle

I will not venture to offer any justifiable reasoning as to the self-destructive behaviors plaguing black and brown America. The elements of crime in America's inner cities, in many ways can be viewed as self-genocide, horrendously damaging the evolutionary progression of our culture. This self-extinctive mind-set, fueled by the drug culture and seemingly senseless acts of street violence serves as a sad commentary on our social and moral condition. However, we must also consider the basic instincts created through the processes of social and psychological conditioning.

The socioeconomic experiment that is the American criminal justice/injustice system has succeeded in devising a maze of circumstances and conditions that in effect guide the feeders of the system into a vicious social and psychological trap. Picture the life of all too many black and brown youth. Born into the decimating cycle of poverty and substandard education, they grow up into a condensed economy fueled by a brutal and seemingly clandestine drug culture, living in territorial war zones of gang violence, subjected to unbalanced sentencing laws designed to indefinitely incarcerate mostly black men, and under the vigilant eye of law enforcement which exists like that of an occupying force, more so than one of community service. Meanwhile, our military system targets and attracts the poor and underprivileged of American society, influencing the idea that few other options exist other than a career as a soldier.

These conditions, in addition to the moral and spiritual divisions that exist within the black community, are further complicated by the lack of economic ownership and empowerment, assisting in a mind-set of desperation and hopelessness.

All of these elements contribute to the growth and perpetuation of the criminal justice/ injustice entity.

The often unjust warehousing of black men within these complexes indicates a direct contradiction of justice and rehabilitation in America and is reminiscent of another time when black men, women and children were entrapped, bought and sold into an institution that held them captive as cheap labor to fuel an economic system. Ultimately, they're left with little to no viable options of social or cultural mobility to advance themselves or their culture.

Today's flavor of justice for black and brown America is an element of suppression; if left unobstructed, it will continue to adversely alter the evolutionary development of an entire culture.

While we as Black people must be mindful and conscious of our own tendencies of self-destructive behaviors and actions, we must be even more mindful that today's criminal justice/injustice system is slavery anew; invisible chains are still chains.

The Educational System

Either by accident, intent or incompetence America's educational system as it relates to black and other minority youth is a grossly failed test. Schools futilely attempt to educate and prepare the young people of our society to ascend to a higher level of mobility within the American economic and social structure.

From Pre-School to the Penitentiary:
A Candid Examination of a Vicious Cycle

In fact, our educational system is the tattletale on American cultural and societal development. It is a microcosm of our failures as a society and is as strategically biased as the playing field of the so-called "American Dream." Our educational system mimics our historical legacy of suppression of knowledge and of our depravation of the mental expansion to dream beyond our immediate comprehension.

In recent years, the "No Child Left Behind" initiative of the former Bush administration was yet another pretense by the federal government. Remaining as an ironic contradiction of its own mantra the initiative exists as a corrupt numbers racket within the educational systems displaying an empty attempt to justify its nonexistent progress. Other efforts include those by local school districts, which are the immediate overseers of federal and state systems and policies. In most cases—if we are to assess them according to their own measurements such as graduation and dropout rates and test scores—local schools have been inept in their levels of expertise to educate the many diverse segments of our society and corrupt within their systems of reward and discipline.

Instead of demonstrating their ability to succeed educationally, Black children are discriminately fed into the alternative school system that includes remediation, detention and "special" education, where they are treated and conditioned as prisoners—placing them one step closer to the larger industrialized prison complexes of American society. In these alternative systems they are slammed, beaten, thrown into large concrete rooms with soundproof doors and guarded throughout their day, often by local police armed with guns, mace and taser weapons. Often, these children are unjustly medicated to keep them "at bay" and "docile" for the benefit of alternative schools' administrative and teaching staffs.

The disproportionate population of black children in the alternative system, as opposed to their white counterparts, speaks to the biased philosophies and policies of these educational institutions. By proportion, black children are far more inadequate in their reading and math skills, fed far more frequently into the alternative school system, and have a lower graduation rate and a higher dropout rate than their white schoolmates.

Ideologically, our educational institutions are supposedly a way out for the downtrodden and underprivileged of our society. Students, parents and educators at schools housing poor and minority youth have believed that an education is a social equalizer to the economic chasm of American culture. This ideology has proven to be true for some who have seeped through the cracks of the system and a number of examples exist among black achievers whose educational background boosted their accomplishments. To our greater misfortune, though, economic biases and social injustices of the system itself cast a shadow of hopelessness upon the hearts and minds of many black, brown and poor youth. The end results in far too many cases have led them into the prison system, unemployment, homelessness, and into a military machine which stands upon the shoulders of those who exist at the lowest rung of the American social and economic ladder.

I am not stating that all of our ills are to be laid at the feet of America's educational system. However, I am stating that this system is corrupt in its practices, inadequate in its outreach strategies and far too often, detrimental to the aspirations of black, brown and poor children.

From Pre-School to the Penitentiary:
A Candid Examination of a Vicious Cycle

Statistical paperwork called IEPs (Individual Education Programs) as well as other paper trails create the appearance of a genuine outreach strategy for our children. Far too often, these strategies are no more than camouflage. They attempt to justify outreaches that are halfhearted in their efforts. If attempted at all, the strategies can often backfire and fail due to lack of follow-up, absence of embedded involvement by parents, caregivers and other community members, and an arrogant belief that school officials and other "experts" know best how to conduct outreach.

This speaks volumes to the social and psychological oppression of a people and indicates a systematic design that does not take into account the positive mobility of black children.

Theoretically, America's educational systems are meant to be a catalyst designed to serve all men, women and children of our society. Attending school is supposed to advance people to various levels of personal, social and economic fulfillment. But in reality, black, brown and poor people discover that the theory of our educational system is consistent with the uncompromising futility and struggle to attain fulfillment of the American Dream. Its very ideology is born from the oppression of black children and adults who, through slavery, were beaten and killed for reading books and striving for literacy. After emancipation, they were segregated from white children and given the scraps of educational and learning environments. Eventually; school desegregation came under the wrath of racist, violent protesters, apathetic or disapproving government officials, and chants of death from the Ku Klux Klan.

Trends

In today's non-productive and suppressive system of education, black children once again find themselves at the lowest rung on the educational ladder.

This cycle is especially vicious in that it creates perpetually reoccurring lowered productivity related to the potential of black children, whose horizons have shrunk and who might pass along lowered expectations to their children when they eventually become black adults and ultimately, black parents. Without the legacy of success throughout the educational process, lowered self-worth and lowered expectations are doomed to be repeated.

Black children are the undeserving causalities of the American system of education, and those watch and do nothing are as guilty as the architects and caretakers of that system.

The educational injustices that exist in America today involve an intentional design to create a perpetual underclass of our society. This is nothing more than modern slavery by way of a cruel, racist and calculating hierarchy which thinks nothing more of our children's future than to assure that their attainment of a greater mobility remains forever immobile.

The Community

For most black, brown and poor youth in America, the conditions of their community exist as a wasteland of poverty and despair. Most poverty stricken communities are ravaged with drugs, violent crime, prostitution, gangs, and a detrimental presence of police and criminal justice.

From Pre-School to the Penitentiary:
A Candid Examination of a Vicious Cycle

Another important element that these communities generally share is that they possess no power base with which to tangibly improve on the dilapidated conditions of their surroundings. Instead, power is imposed by external forces, groups and individuals. Many of these communities have been infiltrated by an outside presence which owns virtually all of the businesses— what few types exist, since in many poor neighborhoods businesses consist mainly of blocks of vacant lots, a few nail/hair salons, liquor and convenience stores, and in rare instances, supermarkets. These and other businesses earn the highest monetary capital available in these areas. These practices result in a depletion of community capital that is earned within the community and an influx of capital taken out of the community and invested far beyond the confines of the community itself.

In a nation where black children are three times more likely as white children to be born into the vicious cycle of poverty and four times more likely as white children to live and exist in extreme poverty, we must strive to fully understand the destructive process of this social and psychological dilemma.[4]

Community conditions are extremely relevant to the development, be it positive or negative, of any culture's growth processes. These conditions greatly influence the evolutionary progression which determines the life mobility of individual elevation or dissension.

Many inner city communities throughout America, due to the extreme violence and heavy loss of life, are statistically categorized as "war zones" where inhabitants suffer from Post-Traumatic Stress Disorder just the same as those within any war torn nation around the world.

Trends

The children of these ravaged communities still must make themselves available for school while attempting to live within a perception of normalcy. They're asked to act as though their setting is like that of children in America existing outside of their environment who rarely if ever experience extreme violence, a debilitating drug culture and abject poverty. These adverse conditions negatively impact upon the moral compass and developmental mind-set which influences relationships, self-image, responsibility, respectability, commitment, and aspiration.

Remarkably, poor and minority youth have another factor bearing down on them: the counterclockwise spin of the "status quo" who generally view the onset and currency of these conditions as being the fault and sole responsibility of those who exist within these adversely challenging environments. In many cases, the managers of this spin fail to comprehend that they have become an adversary of the downtrodden. Some have served as the architects, landlords and policy makers of these communities yet they fail to hold themselves accountable for the impact afflicting our youth.

These cycles of social and economic underdevelopment are structurally relevant to the prevailing mind-set of those who dwell within these environments. The rules of engagement as they relate to the production of individual successes and failures are skewed to adapt to the adverse terrain of the community itself. Violent crime, underachievement in the educational arena, gang life mentalities, low self-image and a diminished motivational mind-set are destructive cornerstones in communities that possess no structural power base to map an escape from their plight. Housing projects, chemical plants, underdeveloped business districts, low performing schools, the spiritual and moral stagnation of the church, the profusion of liquor stores, and an occupying police presence effectively suppress the predominately black and brown people of these communities.

Ultimately, these suppressive conditions spin into the larger cycle of social depravation, inevitably producing populations of unemployed and uneducated people who are ill equipped to construct institutions that preserve family-oriented, neighborly and child-directed environments. Instead, suppressive conditions in poverty stricken communities assist in perpetuating counterproductive and destructive behaviors that transform young black males into feeders of the criminal justice and industrialized prison complexes of America.

The misguided rants of the "pull yourself up by your own bootstraps" mentality that is so often spoken by those who exist beyond the realm of this vicious cycle do not comprehend the basic cause and effect from which the condition itself was initially created. The architects of this sociological experiment, who have designed and imposed these oppressive conditions which adversely impact the whole of our culture, have sought to relinquish any responsibility for contributing to the developmentally downward spiral of an entire generation.

Social and environmental conditions are relevant in not only their design and implementation; these conditions exist within the hearts and minds of a people who would otherwise seek to alter the matrix of a counterproductive and oppressive design. The plight of the Black community is as much a mind-set as it is a tangible living condition.

Trends

It appears that the survival instincts of the Black community are skewed and adaptive to a non-expansive cycle of counterproduction and low level of expectation. Still, there lies a much deeper cause and effect relationship in this dilemma. As with any sociological experimentation, there is the residual effect from the psychological and environmental perspective. None of this happened overnight. Generations of tinkering, planning, budgeting, and other details of so-called "help" have gone into the outcome known as the "inner city" or the "ghetto."

The environmental maze of abject poverty, drug culture, failed schools, violent rage and other criminal activity seemingly offers no avenue of escape. These conditions perpetually diminish the mind-set of productive choice, influencing the initial cycle to transform into what becomes commonly accepted as the cultural norm. While many have escaped from these adversarial conditions, the maze that is the community itself still remains. The tenants of these ravaged communities—less empowered now than ever before—tend to greatly underestimate the arrogance of American ideology and its calculating and oppressive history of social and psychological manipulation. They may recognize their communities are ravaged and "the white man" is to blame, but the degree to which brown and black residents of poverty stricken communities perceive of these conditions as a characteristic standard-bearer of our present-day culture remains unknown.

If they knew how arrogant, calculating and oppressive American ideology was and is, it begs the question of why black and brown people allow these conditions to continue and seem to do nothing productive about their current increase. Self-determination would seem to be an answer which has yet to emerge.

These conditions which have become the norm of American sociological design and implementation exist through a culture entrenched within the repetition of oppression and low level expectation. The matrix of the injustices within black neighborhoods is altered only within the confines of its own design; manifested through the elements of a hostile systematic economic and psychological takeover. Ruinous acts of manipulation and murder define its direction. At its current rate of existence, the road ahead seems predicated by a people's weakened and misguided will, whose desire and faith to transcend their condition seems as ravaged as the environment in which they live.

Family Structure and History

The family structure and history of black people in America exists as a cohesive element in determining the positive evolution of our culture. Family has been our cornerstone and our foundation, existing throughout the history of a cruel and uncompromising social hierarchy.

The unity of the black family is essential to establishing its capability in transcending the often empty embrace of American society, and while societal efforts throughout American history have continued to disrupt and divide, black families have succeeded to some extent in compromising its elevation and development. Black families have persevered in embracing their own vision of unity and empowerment.

However, from a socially developmental and economic perspective, black families exist within a state of crisis, inhibiting our capacity to expand beyond our current condition. This curtails our ascension within the twisted framework of American sociology.

Various elements within the family structure and its history contribute to the cycle of development. Psychologically, there is a level of conditioning consistent with the behavior patterns exhibited within a generational context. Whether this conditioning is attributed to work and labor, criminality, motivation, responsibility, abusive behavior, and the like, the negative aspects of this cycle are sometimes broken. But these instances are the exception more so than the rule.

The sociological and cultural development of one's family structure and its history is as a cascade of life events that shape and process its eventual actuality and reality. Sociological and cultural conditioning is relevant on every level of one's personal and interactive development. One does what they have most commonly perceived to be their catalyst to become upwardly mobile within an environment.

Speaking directly of our youth, who have been and are diminished in their optional development to excel within this social structure of ours, their families' structures are most commonly those of "survival" as opposed to "social climbing". Their ceilings of achievement are set to a perceived "lower standard" as opposed to what is viewed as "acceptable" by the most common

From Pre-School to the Penitentiary:
A Candid Examination of a Vicious Cycle

societal perceptions. Many of them have not, or have settled for the basic goal of graduating from high school. But being a people of great inner strength and pride, many have gone further to expand upon their realm of life options and possibilities.

The ultimate goal from the perspective of the black, brown and poor family in America is to embark on the conditioning process of transcending the negative tapestry of many of their environments. The realization of our great divide must become the catalyst of our unification.

There are many social and environmental conditions that are contributors to our current state of developmental stagnation. The prevailing theme of most black families in today's America is that of a fractured structure of the two-parent household; most often, the mother is the primary caregiver and role model of the family. Many black men, due to their own negative perceptive values of self-worth, are not fully embracing the concept of cohesiveness in a family structure. In addition, there are black men who possess innate contention with black women which is intense enough to prevent an ongoing, consistent relationship of monogamy. Still, too many black men have elected to essentially neglect and abandon their offspring and other family members, ultimately leaving their young sons and daughters to fill in the blanks of the black male parent and role model. This breakdown of cohesive family structure is a vital factor in the overall negative development of young black males and females and serves to perpetuate the elements of a vicious cycle of rage, promiscuity, gang loyalty, prison incarceration, and low achievement in the educational arena.

Trends

The relationship roles of the black man and woman through sociological and economical depravation have suffered a drastic emotional and moral breakdown, creating a chasm in their interactive and productive development. While the overall responsibility lies within the re-bonding (if you will) of the black male and female to set and establish the foundations of stronger relationships and mutual respect for each other, there are many factors that contribute to this interactive dissension. These seeds of dissension are deeply rooted within a social and economic pathology that has in effect divided the compatibility between the black male and female in America.

In America today, there are over one million black men currently incarcerated and/or involved within the prison and criminal justice systems. As a result, the mobility of social advancement for the black woman, in comparison, is far greater than that of her black male counterpart.

The educational dropout rate, proportionately, for black men, far exceeds that of any other segment of American society.

As the black male in America approaches social and developmental extinction—due to prison incarceration, lack of education, black-on-black violence, police-on-black violence, and poor health care—the black woman is left to assume the role of mother, father, provider, and role model for our children.

The shortage of cohesive family structures within the culture of black people in America has proven to be a sustaining factor in perpetuating the cycle of our underdevelopment. This scarcity starves the creating of positive relationships, while enhancing attraction to negative and detrimental influences.

From Pre-School to the Penitentiary:
A Candid Examination of a Vicious Cycle

Not to be underestimated are the innate human desires to seek out the affirmations of recognition, acknowledgement and guidance which tend to be much more accessible and nurturing in a cohesive family structure. Many black children born into the often adversarial cycle of American culture are lacking these vitally essential elements. In the void that exists when there are rare instances of cohesive family structures there of abandonment, self-defamation, reckless decision making, and other self-destructive behaviors. These reactions at the early stages of youth development influence the eventual reactive thought and action processes of adult life. The cycle is ultimately left to recreate itself, from generation to generation.

The family structure and history of black people in America speaks to the power and strength of a people to combat and challenge the ideologies of racism and oppression that to this day has an impact on the psychological and productive mind-set that assists in determining the direction, be it positive or negative, of an entire culture and countless generations.

Meanwhile, the involvement of America's influence in creating the reality of this vicious cycle of youth and family development is not to be underestimated. American ideology has very effectively sought to suppress the developmental growth and productive mind-set of an entire race and culture who have survived the annals of slavery, rape, murder, lynching, Jim Crow laws, and today's flavor of bootstrap ideology.

The vestiges of suppression and injustice have not at all vanished from our reality but have, in fact, changed only in their stealthy implementation of prison incarceration, police brutality, substandard education, poor health care, run-down communities economically controlled by outside influences, and a drug culture which masquerades as a job market for our youth.

The assault upon the black, brown and poor family in American is no illusion.

As we grow wiser, we realize the many elements and circumstances of our current condition. We must remain conscious of our own responsibilities and missteps which have also contributed to the creation and maintaining of this vicious cycle.

Our family structure and history is being etched anew each and every day.

We must come to realize that our silence is not "golden" but destructive to the causes of our children and our culture. Our muted voices and our "turn the other cheek" ideologies are in fact destructive to the seeds which we have created. The ceiling of our standards and achievements must be broken and transcended to realize newly expanded possibilities. It lies within our commitment to each other, at this point of our social, moral and family development, to become proactive about what will ultimately determine the strength, longevity and greatness of our children and the whole of our culture.

The American Dream

The harsh reality of the "American Dream" is that of a blatant misconception which manifests the moral and philosophical hypocrisies of our nation.

From Pre-School to the Penitentiary:
A Candid Examination of a Vicious Cycle

It is baffling that the U.S. government—which has come to its lofty presence by way of slavery, war and human conquest—cannot come to realize the moral, sociological, economical, and psychological influences that are indelibly etched within its history.

Here in the 21st century, over 150 years since the so-called abolishment of slavery, the American Dream/Dilemma is alive and well. When directly speaking of the black, brown and poor segments of America society, many still exist within a system of depravation and inequality. Since this so-called abolishment of what we have come to know as chattel slavery, black people in America have in many ways, been kept under America's heel to this very day.

We can identify many examples. Mass lynching of black people in America occurred during and following the advent of slavery, peaking in the early 20th century. The Ku Klux Klan conducted racist, terrorist crusades throughout much of the 20th century with widespread exposure of their criminal activities occurring during the Civil Rights Movement. This movement often focused on suppression of voting rights in the South which put blacks and their supporters in physical danger. The Black Codes—laws passed by southern states in 1865 in an attempt to regain control over blacks after the Civil War— school segregation throughout the U.S. and its violent aftermath of school desegregation after the Supreme Court ruling in 1954 are other examples of society's efforts to maintain slave-like treatment of blacks. Present-day racial profiling and police brutality remain as staples of the American process.

Trends

These examples are provided to highlight the lasting effects upon an entire race of people as they relate to the sociological and psychological levels of conditioning.

Have there been societal advancements to assist in rectifying many of these gross injustices?

Yes.

However, these advancements do not relieve or extinguish the engrained thought processes of inferiority, rage and rebellion etched within the consciousness of black adults and children alike.

The American Dream for black, poor and other minority youth is an unrealistic mantra that imposes a false sense of probability within a system designed to use these youth as fuel to maintain an unjust and biased political and social order. These children fuel the prison systems of America, maintain the much needed poverty levels of a capitalistic society, feed an inadequate educational system, and prop up a military machine—all the while advancing and protecting economic interests of the rich and powerful of our society.

What cannot be ignored are the adverse levels of psychological conditioning inflicted on these children by way of a historically corrupt, racist and oppressive ideology prevalent since the inception of America itself. "Old money" as it is often referred to, is money accumulated by businesses that thrived in the early times of America and have been left to their ancestors today. Businesses such as CSX and Norfolk Southern Railroads, Aetna and New York Life Insurance and educational institutions such as Harvard, Yale and Brown University all have capitalized and profited from the lives and deaths of Black people through the institution of slavery.

Black people as slaves received no compensation for their toil. Many of their ancestors live and dwell in abject poverty and oppression in America today, while the families owning these institutions—such as the Vanderbilts, the Carnegies, the Du Ponts, and the Rockefellers—are rich and powerful in this country. Their "American Dream" came to fruition by way of the nightmare and suffering of black people. There are many other instances such as these in America, which exemplify the seeds of oppression and injustice and have left us to question the validity and the sincerity of the American Dream.

None of our children have "old money" with which to start anew or invest in their future. They grow up impoverished and must struggle for survival each day of their lives. We do have examples of those whose rise from history is great, even though their exploits are strategically left out of the American conversation—we get mere scraps of instances when there are likely to be more.

The hierarchy of American sociological ideology and implementation exists as a self-serving vision of the American Dream which states that any expectation of accomplishment in our land can be realized with hard work and an undying faith in the American creed—pull yourself up by your bootstraps, you can have life, liberty and the pursuit of happiness, and so on. But consciously or unconsciously the American Dream becomes an experience of balancing or unbalancing the dimensions of the dream for those who have been and are socially, spiritually and psychologically compromised in their toil to bring to fruition, the reality of that dream. The dream concept is distorted within its own mechanics, drastically skewing its eventual outcome and adversely affecting those, who by a divisive design, must adapt to realize their "American Dream" in an uncompromising, reverse order. That is, the "American Dream" scenario is delusional—beginning at a radically unequal level of adversity, as opposed to an optimal level of a far less conflicting avenue of ascending choices.

While it exists within the realm of possibility that one can overcome obstacles on virtually any level, while possible, is a host of blatant contradictions in that its fruition exists at the other end of a diametrically opposed spectrum of real probabilities.

Our reality, as opposed to the American Dream is the intentional implementation of a variety of misguided concepts bred within misconception and based on an empty theory of attainability, regardless of one's dire circumstances.

The American Dream is a process of attrition for not only our youth, but for all of black, brown and poor America. Our lacking of the realization of self has been the most profound detriment to the access of our greatness.

As it has been proven, black people in America can indeed pursue and reach the highest levels of our society. Diligence and determination are intrinsic within our history. Attainability dwells not only within the justice and consciousness of a nation, but also within the faith, vision and inner strength of a people to overcome the obstacles of a preconditioned society. Lacking the magic of imagination and the realm of possibilities, this society's predilections are geared toward those, who by their own misguided perception are unlike their true selves.

Systematic Factors

The Church

The historical commentary of the church and its developmental concept of religious expression possesses a history that is rich in its teaching and powerful in its outreach.[5]

The unprecedented ability of the church to unite its masses through spirituality and faith to effect positive change in a world that most commonly appears to have lost its sense of morality stands as one of its greatest achievements.

Many churches stand as cornerstones in a host of impoverished and so-called higher risk communities; providing many with much needed assistance. Those troubled by drugs, the homeless, families needing day care services or food are among those receiving youth and family developmental outreach services and mentorship provisions to the young—be they gang related or college bound.

In addition, from an individual perspective, the church has been an eternal source of inner strength to challenge and conquer life's obstacles on a variety of levels. There remains no doubt that the church entity has been an agent of liberation through times of abject struggle. For far too many churches, however, this legacy has been tarnished by the arrogance and hypocrisy of a people and a nation entrenched within their own misguided ideology.

Systematic Factors

Among industrialized nations, America is among the most adverse in violent crime, health care, prison incarceration, the death penalty, education, drug addiction, and infant mortality. Yet there are many churches whose basic tenets and ministries seem to have lost their way when it comes to compassion and activism. These churches tend to perceive of addicts, ex-cons, teen parents, runaways, and others as sinners who are too sinful to help. At these churches, activism—a relentless pursuit of justice, empowerment and an authentic realization of self-determination—tends to occur outside the church's walls, not within its congregation. Curiously, this was not the case during prior eras of the black faith tradition. Examples focusing on just one denomination include:

- The early years of the Emanuel African Methodist Episcopal Church of Charleston, SC in the 1800s;[6]

- Bishop Henry McNeal Turner, first southerner to become an AME bishop and one of a group of African Americans to become elected officials of state and federal government during Reconstruction;[7]

- Richard Allen, a founder of the AME Church, a denomination begun in 1787 after white congregants refused to allow blacks to pray and participate in church services, citing "religious assembly" laws of the late 1700s banning blacks from attending church.[8]

As the above examples and other instances indicate, the righteousness of any religious order is determined through the conscious intent and actions of its people. Far too often, today's church is a facade of its own ideology and philosophy, relying more on its rhetoric than in its production.

One may perceive that the power of religious spirituality through the church would seek to transcend its arrogance; challenging the social and moral injustices of our nation. What we find, however, is a stagnated power base, seemingly content with the glowing legacy of its past. The productive powers of our spirituality and inner strength are jeopardized when there are the misguided perceptions among those who have compromised their faith, between God and man-made ideology.

In one of my previous works *Inner Strength Defies the Skeptic* (Immediex, 2006) in the section titled "Faith" I state: "While man-made ideologies have us reaching for faith through corrupt teaching and confrontational misunderstanding, we are being robbed and misdirected of our own untapped power."

This statement was intended to exemplify the arrogant ideology of mankind as it relates to our lack of transcendence beyond our own destructive levels of religious and spiritual comprehension.

The church's role as a cornerstone of the black community seems to have lost its basic vision of unity and empowerment. Black churches are increasingly unable to grasp the hopes of a people and bring to bear the power of the oppressed masses through the unity of spirituality and faith. This unused power, if tapped and appropriately targeted, combats the oftentimes oppressive ideologies of an unrelenting system that has been and is detrimental to the causes of black people and ultimately all of America.

Our inability or willful failure to separate our inner strength from the "bricks and mortar" facility that is the "church" has compromised our developmental capabilities to transcend negativity and overcome our current state of mental and spiritual stagnation.

Perhaps we should take into account the religious missteps of a people, as opposed to the inadequacies of an institution; that is, the church. By mimicking the characteristics of American society and clothing itself in grand prosperity, the church has compromised the sincerity of its intent. Many churches stand as elaborate structures in the heart of economically deprived communities; ministers live in lavishness, far beyond the scope of those they are supposedly "called" to serve. These symbols contradict the message to the masses that greed is wrong. In contrast, parishioners are told that all which transpires in one's life is "God's will" as if one should be content with their plight, regardless of the circumstances.

Our children ultimately suffer, as they seek guidance on a myriad of levels in communities where the church is one of the few existing places where youth can go, seeking help with basic needs and internal struggles.

Many youth have witnessed tragedies and experienced traumatic situations. To see the family of a murder victim, have a drug addicted mother, know a child killed in crossfire or a father's shame of poverty is beyond what many a soldier must bear during wartime. Perhaps more tragic, though, is to be told this is the will of God when instead it is perhaps the will of men who are not of God.

The lofty presence that is equated with the church is frequently misplaced, in that it holds to its highest reverence a human being and a structural entity that are only as powerful as the faith of its inhabitants. The preachers and ministers of the church are perhaps no more spiritually enlightened than any human being who would be born into the wilderness. They embrace a faith within that which is unseen by the physical eye, but whose works are manifest in amazing and glorifying fashion.

We have chosen to elevate these individuals to a status that is almost God-like in our expression. The unified power of our faith is compromised due to our individual inability or unwillingness to realize the capacities of our own beliefs and inner strength.

We have neglected our responsibility to those who are seemingly beyond our grasp and who exist within the depravation of our society.

In addition, the outreach strategies of many churches are virtually nonexistent as they relate to embracing those who are at highest risk or are among those who are more highly exposed to the societal and cultural dilemmas of our time.

The churches' leadership, through its production, has not stood at the forefront to unite the masses—be they of the church entity, or not—to rebel against the injustices of a nation in denial. The power and influence of the church and its capability to stand against American injustice should be essential to its purpose and its existence. Instead, we find church leaders standing in the background—as mute yet present apologists or "yes men" for officials who line pastors' pockets with cash as long as they "put up and shut up." To live one's life in search of a reward for one's "good" deeds—is this not the ultimate act of selfishness?

Perhaps the most intriguing element of churches' misdirection exists within its structural teaching and guidance of our children. What messages are we sending them as they seek guidance on the spiritual and moral aspects of life? At what points are we teaching them about peaceful nonviolence, about how to produce oratory which speaks truth to injustice and powerful influences, about organizing that holds elected officials and others in America's elite accountable for their inaction and mistreatment? When do churches even educate young people about Bishops Allen and Turner, Mother Emanuel AME Church, and other heroic highlights within a church's own history? The pronouncing of our religious faith certainly does not reflect on the production of our works.

We live hypocritically, according to our own religious perceptions, and use the loophole of our weaknesses to justify our ineptitude.

There are churches on practically every street corner in black America, but the manifestation of their works through faith is virtually nonexistent.

Perhaps we should seek to realize that the essence of the church is not about the structure built around us; instead, the essence consists of the structure built within us.

What Is
The Awareness Project?

The Awareness Project is the basic foundation and symbolic reference to all of my work.

It is the common denominator which encompasses all of my theoretical, philosophical, sociological, psychological, and creative expression.

The name "The Awareness Project" as well as its slogan "within the seed of an apple there lives an orchard invisible" creatively serves to encompass my basic vision of positive growth through realization of self as well as an Awareness of ones sociological and psychological conditions.

Existing as more of a conceptual outreach program, which focused more on design and implementation. The Awareness Project is not a structural entity located in any specific location;

The Awareness Project reaches out to all facets of people regardless of age, social class, racial or religious background.

Since its inception, in 1995, The Awareness Project has been an active participant in a vast array of arenas; raging from lectures, seminars, motivation, consultations, community mobilization, gang intervention, and staff development trainings.

The Awareness Project has organized and challenged individuals, families, groups, and communities from predominately the Greater Louisville, Ky. and surrounding areas and as far south as Alabama to address issues and concerns relative to the positive development and uplifting of their lives.

What Is The Awareness Project?

No arena is too large or too small for the powerful message of The Awareness Project.

Each new literary release from The Awareness Project illustrates a new conceptual outreach, intended to enhance people's thinking process by presenting bold philosophical, psychological, theoretical, artistic, motivational, and societal concepts that serve as a catalyst for the development of positive perception and implementation.

The Awareness Project's vision is to enlighten and empower individuals, families, groups, institutions, and communities to:

- Achieve a greater sense of self-worth;

- Realize the constructive power of positive perception and action;

- Understand the development of and how to engage positive and negative cycles;

- Positively develop and enhance the productive powers of the inner self, while maintaining a desire and thirst for knowledge.

Conditions

Community Empowerment

Among the many devastations that have been leveled upon the cultural development of black people in America, the systematic ravages of the black community are among the greatest.

Worse still, our ineptitude in seizing and possessing the power base that is the black community has proven to be a detriment to our elevation as a culture.

Community empowerment is quite simplistic in theory but is improbable in its fruition.

In examining the status of the black community you generally find a stolen and co-opted power base, infiltrated by those who exist and reside outside of the community itself. This process features the intention to diminish black culture and people's worth by weakening symbols of authority and influence and downgrading expressions of artistry—all of which motivate and unify people—and replacing these with expressions, "leaders" and symbols without authentic value.

Let's look at the economic side of this issue. There exists within the black community a broken economy, serving the economic interests of primarily of Middle Eastern, Caucasian, Asian and Jewish backgrounds. This reality is devastating to the black community. While there are black-owned businesses in black neighborhoods, many of them are run from broken-down storefronts, dilapidated garages, or street corner set ups. Meanwhile their counterparts run their establishments from newer buildings and often have additional operations set in various locations throughout the community itself, indicating the existence of more capital and greater financial stability than is the case among many black-owned businesses.

While liquor stores, pawn shops, check cashing institutions, convenience stores, fast food types of restaurants and nail and hair salons are the dominant establishments within the black community, this is due to our uncompromising loyalty to these businesses and it profoundly demonstrates our lack of understanding and implementation of community empowerment.

As black people are the dominant population within their own communities, it would serve in our best interest to utilize our dominance as leverage to assure that all businesses within the black community serve to some extent the basic ideology of uplifting the black community as a whole. In addition, those who are the black community should not patronize any establishment that does not assist in supporting and uplifting the black community.

Our youth exist within their communities with no jobs, substandard housing and few avenues to advance themselves. Yet black community leaders are virtually silent and invisible in their efforts to enhance the economic and social mobility of those who are the black community. We find various other cultures infiltrating the black community for financial gain and future stability for their families—with bank loans, revenue invested by family members, and trade associations mobilized and united in their tasks. Those who are the black community seem to be vastly divided in their unity to mobilize and organize themselves to establish their future stability and to empower themselves to establish a foundation of positive mobility for themselves, their families and the community as a whole.

There are many factors that lead to a divided black community. These factors are culturally divisive, as they relate to a conditioning process during and following the advent of slavery. In those days slave owners pitted us against each other for the most basic goals of survival. Ironically, the "Willie Lynch Doctrine" continues to serve as the template of our demise. Those who were the community organizers of their time—including Harriet Tubman, Sojourner Truth, Frederick Douglass, and Nat Turner among others—were ostracized by whites and some blacks for their efforts. They were hunted like animals; and often tortured and murdered for their causes.

In the 1960s the community organizers included: the Black Panther Party, Malcolm X, SNCC, Angela Davis, Medgar Evers, Martin Luther King, Jr., and Fred Hampton, the Nation of Islam, and others. They were victimized by those who promoted, supported and perpetuated oppression and injustice in America. Many of them also were assassinated or imprisoned.

The community organizers of today, by way of a discordant strategy, remain as adversaries of a skewed perception of the "American Way" and just as in the past they exist as an undesirable element of the American landscape.

It appears that organizing for community empowerment involves a certain amount of sacrifice due to the effort to articulate and prompt real change.

Conditions

One of the most basic elements required to establishing empowerment within any social structure is mobilization. Mobilization is the development and implementation of a unified vision and purpose, shared and embraced by those involved. This process is targeted toward the tangible as well as the intangible conditions which adversely impact the societal, economic and psychological mobility of our community.

Conditions to focus on include:

- Inability to thrive,

- Unjust community police presence,

- Run down housing,

- Excess of liquor stores,

- High crime and violence,

- Inadequate educational and recreational facilities,

- Too few black-owned businesses,

- Low esteem as a community as shown by loud or aggressive behavior on the street, disarray (bottles and garbage strewn on sidewalks and vacant lots), etc.

These are all factors relevant to the developmental process of mobilizing a community.

One of many conditions that serves to inhibit the mobilization process is the onset and implementation of "Black Flight." This is somewhat different than "White Flight," which was and is a tool of racial segregation present in many American cities. The political hierarchy of many American inner cities, along with many of its white citizens, determined that living with or near a community of black people was not only considered to be substandard living but was seen as detrimental to the well-being of white families and an economic liability to the city and community itself. "White Flight" was instrumental in the process of razing many black-owned homes in America's inner cities and contributed to the beginning of what is now recognized as the "Projects" in many black communities throughout America.

While the factors that contributed to the onset of "White Flight" were blatantly racist; "Black Flight" is relevant from a slightly different perspective. "Black Flight" is a process of social segregation used by black people. Instead of remaining in the black community, participants in "Black Flight" elect to leave the perceived conditions of adversity for a choice seen as in the better interest of themselves and their families. Fair housing laws and improved incomes by some blacks have been factors allowing this process to occur. "Black Flight" is a perceived element of escape from the adversarial conditions of poverty, crime and violence which are commonly equated with all-black, urban neighborhoods.

The effect of "Black Flight" on the black community as a whole is devastating to the process of a long-term commitment by its inhabitants to eradicate the adverse conditions of the community with economic, social and psychological investments. When people invest their money, time, emotions, energy, and expertise in a neighborhood they mean to stay and commit to a real sense of home for themselves, their families and their neighbors.

Conditions

However, "Black Flight" results in an elevated turnover of residents who perhaps do not possess the heightened level of concern to improve on their immediate as well as their long-term conditions. Unfortunately, many residents of black communities become conditioned to their environment and instead of seeking to change the conditions, they accept the conditions and adapt to the terrain in which they live.

Community empowerment is an elusive and complex strategy. Its fruition depends not just on the realization of a diminished capacity to improve upon and transcend the elements of one's surroundings. Community empowerment requires the mental and spiritual capacity to recognize the elements of oppression, injustice and self-depravation that continue to infest the motivational mind-set and morality of an entire culture.

Someone pursuing improvements in their physical well-being must acknowledge the need to make changes—in food choices and exercise, perhaps—that require sacrifice, strain and stretching beyond the present existence to realize goals and sustain improvement. Likewise, community empowerment will require hard-nosed acknowledgment, sacrifice and faithful stretching to accomplish betterment for everyone.

Outreach: Intangibles

Conducting outreach to engage poor and minority youth in empowering their productive development will challenge adults and groups. In addition to elements more typically associated with programs—such as budget, staff, evaluation, etc.—there are important intangible elements to consider and implement. Four intangibles are featured here: atmospheric, inner development/ self-realization, leadership, and accountability.

Atmospheric

Much as our ecological and environmental conditions adjust in their ebb and flow to adapt to atmospheric changes the same holds true for behavioral and productive patterns of our society and more specifically, our youth. Atmospheric conditions and their dynamics can significantly influence patterns of behavior and productivity, leading to growth or stagnation or decline among youth.

At one end of this atmospheric spectrum of context, we have conditions of escalating youth violence, drug usage and dealing, gang activity, high rates of teen pregnancy, a growing population of single-parent households, an overwhelming school dropout rate, and an alarming growth in youth prison incarceration. At the opposite end of this spectrum exists a blatant disdain for authority, epidemic drug usage, an escalating suicide rate and intentional acts of catastrophic violence inflicted upon many of our educational institutions. Both ends of the atmospheric spectrum of our youth's development are, in many ways, essentially counterproductive.

To understand this apparent counterproductive mind-set among many of our youth, we must examine the environmental structure in which our youth live and develop, as it relates to specific adaptations resulting from adults' actions, such as our deficiency in setting positive examples to create and dictate the climate of our communities and our nation.

As adults and youth professionals, we have created for our youth an atmosphere of broken promises and blatant hypocrisy. Essentially we have cast our youth into a whirlwind of doubt, confusion and uncertainty. In many communities throughout America, our youth exist in single-parent environments. They're often reared by only the mother and very often, an aging grandparent. The nuclear, two-parent family has virtually become a thing of the past. The absence of a father's ongoing, consistent presence has created a void in terms of guidance, love and encouragement for youth's development. This void becomes a critically influential factor as male children and adolescents embark on experiences that require help from male adults.

Far too many of our youth are embarking at an early age on a decision making process which defies their maturity.

Budget cuts and reduced financial assistance from foundations have resulted in fewer resources for youth. Productive inner city community centers for our youth are increasingly becoming few and far between, depriving our youth of vital recreation and positive interactive development. Another resource would seem to be available among churches. However, when it comes to black churches, this seems to be a resource for females of all ages more than occurs among young males. Females tend to fill the pews; other than the pastor and elders, there often exists an absence of males at church. Our churches have become far too selective in their clientele and have in essence become more and more detached from our communities.

As for our educational system, while attempting to educate our youth in the conventional arenas of reading, writing and arithmetic, schools have little to no expertise in concepts relating to inner developmental among youth. Our schools have in a sense become no more than a day care system for our youth and a prerequisite to entry into the industrialized prison complex. Schools seem intent on mimicking penal systems' basic ideologies of punishment and judgmental attitudes that presume guilt. Meanwhile, the relationship between our youth and adults has diminished to a point of virtual nonexistence.

The community's past embrace and mentorship of youth mentorship has been replaced by disdain and abandonment by adults. The uplifting and supportive structure that should be exemplified in service of our youth has nearly disappeared. These environmental conditions adversely influence the basic characteristics of one's social, spiritual and psychological instincts that remain vital to the evolution of any culture.

The unfortunate consequences resulting from these current conditions of youth outreach, development and support serve to further entrench themselves into young people's developmental psyche and inevitability produce counterproductive expectations and results.

Outreach: Intangibles

Amid the American social structure, there exists a wide chasm relative to the attainment of upward mobility and sociological ascension. This widening chasm is consistent with the diametrically opposed thought processes which divide the intended unified philosophies of our nation.

What we have in America is a skewed perception of survival and developmental instincts, which are adaptive to the conditions of each individual segment of our society. This apparent polarization of structural ideologies enacts psychological influences that serve to create the totality of our societal structure. This in turn perpetuates the divisions that exist to manifest our current atmosphere of dissension and confrontation among youth and between youth and adults.

Specifically speaking of the black, brown and poor children in America, their atmospheric conditions in many instances are that of a fractured social environment perpetuated by the adaptive influences of extreme violence and other counterproductive cycles. Many times the psychological influences to escape from such conditions are great. However, the preconditioned influences to adapt to one's immediate surroundings are often greater and serve to dominate the ultimate direction of the individual.

The larger segments of our society tend to have shortsighted perceptive values about youths' atmospheric condition. While scoping the environmental conditions of those who exist within these crime infested and drug riddled areas, people tend to denounce not only the immediate conditions of the environment, but the life actions of those who live there. Our youth duly notice the criticism, which increases their motivation to push back. Lacking the tools to do otherwise, their reaction tends to serve self-destructive impulses and black-on-black violence. All this feeds the environment of counterproductivity.

These prevailing conditions, created and implemented by the designers and caretakers of an oppressive system, are entrenched within the elements of racism and class defined ideologies. To some extent adults have relinquished any responsibility to the cause and effect that has now become a liability on the American landscape.

As atmospheric and environmental conditions are relevant to the productive consciousness of any individual, or culture, it is ultimately the responsibility of that individual or culture to extricate or elevate themselves beyond the confines of counterproduction.

The disenfranchised youth of America are confronted with a unique dilemma as they remain entrenched within a dichotomy of power and privilege which masquerades as the standard-bearer of what defines success and failure within the American cultural philosophy. How they will manage the dilemma known as the American Dream will have significant impact on their development and direction. In the midst of their struggle to become adults in an atmosphere of rejection, racism, poverty, and despair happens by way of a divisive ideology that comes to fruition at the expense of the oppressed and uninitiated. This atmosphere will sustain itself, only as long as the current conditions exist that construct and define its makeup.

One thing is certain: These conditions are spinning out of control.

We must respond to this very real crisis with unified empowerment. We must create authentic, lasting conditions that refuse to accept the empty idiom of the American dialogue while also supporting an atmosphere that embraces a dynamic flow of development, features open-ended dialogue with our youth and readily accepts their legitimacy.

Inner Development/Self-Realization

"The most dehumanizing act of one man to another is the intentional and absolute robbery of the self. To rob one of his faith, his history and his quest to dream is greater than any man-made prison."[9]

When an individual or an entire culture possesses no positive catalyst to elevate themselves from the conditions of social and psychological depravation, they unwittingly reinforce the elements from which the condition itself was initially created. Ultimately, this perpetuates a vicious cycle of negative development and adversely impacts the productivity of present and future generations.

The engrained thought processes of self-hatred and lowered expectations of self which have been cruelly and discriminately inflicted upon black people throughout American history have produced devastating conditions of counterproductive behaviors and actions. The effects of these thought processes greatly compromise the social and psychological elevation of our children and our culture.

42

From Pre-School to the Penitentiary:
A Candid Examination of a Vicious Cycle

Robbed of the necessary elements of self-realization, determination and motivation, one cannot imagine or expand the higher realms of aspiration and accomplishment. It has remained indelibly etched into our psyche to believe that we are in essence our own worst enemy. Contaminated since the advent of slavery, the developmental seed of black people has stunted the positive evolution of an entire race of people. Seemingly in vain we fight for the scraps of a dream draped in misconception and injustice.

Meanwhile, the progression toward building upon the positive perception of the inner self remains as an essential element to the productive evolution of black people.

A restructuring of our outreach strategies must feature a design to uplift the moral, spiritual, sociological, and psychological mind-set of a people. This design must take into account our conditioning to assist in our own demise. Black leadership has failed to inspire the young to transcend the setbacks and examine accomplishments of our past. What exists now in terms of this intangible is usually inadequate.

Presently, our outreach initiatives are consistent with the commonality of American developmental ideology. These initiatives, fundamentally; are not relevant to the realistic needs of the cultural development of black people.

- Substantive analyses of how black and brown people have overcome obstacles in the past;

- In-depth examination of the coordination, critique and follow-up that has occurred during various events such as the Freedom Riders of the 1960s, the court challenges to school segregation's "separate but equal" policies, voter registration during the Civil Rights Movement, and other examples;

- Research into the various efforts at self-realization, such as building schools during Reconstruction, combating the use in Chicago of "Willis Wagons" during school boycotts of the 1970s, and mapping routes and recording movement on the Underground Railroad.

These and other initiatives can embed within youth greater ability to use critical thinking skills, chances to partner with one another on projects, and discovery for themselves the experience of intangible yet concrete outcomes of inner development.

The urgency to establish changes in youths' inner development is upon us. Black-on-black genocide is destroying an entire generation. The drug culture serves to supplement a virtually nonexistent job market. Prison incarceration is erasing the productive mobility of young black men. What had been the empowering influence of the church has stagnated. Our educational system is broken and inept. There is a growing disdain by black adults directed toward black youth. We are experiencing a seemingly perpetual, vicious cycle of non-development within our entire culture.

While it may appear on the surface that black people in America have made great strides in their climb up the social and economic ladder of American society, the reality of some people's progress is deceptive.

Perhaps the most detrimental factor that speaks to this crisis exists within the divisional conditions that are prevalent among the cultural behaviors of black people. The infection of class definition has seeped into the conscious thought processes of black people in America. We have become a divided people, self-segregating by way of economic, class and cultural divisions. Spiritually, we are of diminished faith in our culture's previous reliance on our churches as a sanctuary for all ages. We have become greatly compromised in our capabilities to transform religious rhetoric into reality. Without the bond of previous eras, we remain an empty people, left standing and waiting for an unjust societal hierarchy to dictate and determine our fate and evolution. This, too, can influence the inner development of our youth, who observe adults' lack of proactivity at church—when adults attend—and become cynical about the potential for spiritual growth and empowering self-realization.

As black people in America, many are conditioned to mimic the ways and actions of those who have sought our demise. We have turned a deaf ear to our children and seek no understanding as to their actions and behaviors. We cast them out, turning off their music, criticizing their appearance, and praying they rot in prison for their misguided and seemingly senseless acts of crime and violence.

We fail to realize that our rejection and abandonment of them serves as a catalyst for their desperation. While they grow into an environment drastically compromised of its upward mobility, they search for constructive guidance.

We must engage our youth to choose freedom over incarceration, life over death, family life over gang life, self-fulfillment over self-depravation, education over illiteracy, self-pride over self-hatred, self-respect over self-loathing, self-love over self-destruction, community pride over community shame, and a true seeking of spiritual awareness which involves much more than just going to church.

There is not something missing within the hearts and souls of our children as much as there is something not yet realized.

We as a people must reawaken the search for our own inner strength. When we do, adults will discover a renewed search that benefits their own inner development as we undertake our role in engaging with youth. Our self-realization awaits confirmation by way of the will of a people who know not of the power within their own souls and who have seemingly forgotten the legacy of their own greatness.

Leadership

From the broadest perspective, the more systematic and societal structures of American leadership—such as those relevant to education, criminal justice, the political arena, and the religious sector—exhibit a common logic, demonstrating a dearth of economic and socially developmental strategies designed to equip and uplift the downtrodden and uninitiated of our society.

From Pre-School to the Penitentiary:
A Candid Examination of a Vicious Cycle

The leadership hierarchy in America caters to the advances of the social elite, assuring their exemption from the harsh realities of the political, economic and social order. Meanwhile, those who are most commonly defined by racial and class definition in America, remain as the standard-bearers, upholding an unbalanced doctrine of American social and economic ascension.

The mechanics of American leadership is an intricate mixture of intent and execution. While our leadership doctrine professes to be "by the people and for the people" its execution is deceptive, in that it works primarily in the constructive service of a social hierarchy. But the hierarchy is designed to maintain an uneven balance of power and privilege, creating a vast economic chasm and drastically compromising the upward mobility of America's societal underclass.

When we examine the moral principles and basic character of American leadership, as well as its productive value, we find a legacy entrenched in a dichotomy of racial and class definition.

Racially, the concept and implementation of American leadership is deceptively segregated.

While examining the cause and effect of leadership in America and its representation, we can witness the racial intent and division. Ideally, leadership in America is intended to be in the productive service of all Americans. Its reality is in service of the primary interests of predominately white America.

Ask yourself:

Who are the richest and most privileged in America?

47

Who oversees the highest and most influential levels of political power?

Who dominates educational implementation and law enforcement?

Who are the primary lawmakers and shapers of those laws?

By contrast:

Per capita, Black Americans are among the poorest and most inadequately educated; they possess the highest unemployment rate and the highest infant mortality rate; they are the least healthy and the most incarcerated citizens of American society.[10]

Whether by intent, accident or design, American leadership does not perform in the best interests of all Americans.

The lower tiers resulting from American leadership structure fall into a host of segregated and symbolic categorizations. When someone Black becomes socially prominent in America, he or she is referred to as a "black leader" who represents "black leadership" and a segment of the "black agenda." The same occurs for those of Hispanic or Native American descent. This segmented representation of American leadership also possesses some semblance of productive value, in that its intent is to speak to the social, economic, moral, and spiritual concerns of our society's many diverse segments.

From Pre-School to the Penitentiary:
A Candid Examination of a Vicious Cycle

However, there is much to be achieved in the interim before concept becomes reality. For in as much as American leadership is plagued by racial contention, it is as much burdened by class definition as well.

The hierarchy of American leadership that serves to shape the direction of policy and privilege is skewed to create a limited exemption to many, regardless of race or culture; but more so by one's social and economic status.

By class definition, American leadership is generally indiscriminate as to which segment of our society possesses the most grueling climb up the American ladder of social and economic ascension. It is also important to realize that class definition reaches beyond the boundaries of racial categorization.

Age grouping, educational status, physical and mental health, housing demographics, and economic standing are all factors that contribute to defining class definition by American leadership. Those who remain at the lowest levels of these categorizations, regardless of race, are susceptible to dwell within the cellar of the same cause and effect of America's leadership doctrine.

Among the most damaging elements of this doctrine of American leadership is that it is perpetual and reproductive within its effects. While some seep through the cracks to excel, many adults, families and their children are caught within the cycle and legacy of low achievement, resulting in substandard expectation and productivity. This generational dilemma contributes to maintaining the social and economic underclass, which is consistent with the embodiment of a capitalist society.

Outreach: Intangibles

As our children suffer from this lack of productive leadership on virtually every level of their development, their immediate conditions entice them to mimic their supposed role models. These models include those who have instilled within them a value system whose basic intent is self-serving in its aim and essentially non-productive in its implementation as it relates to the positive mobility of any culture.

Our passivity as a people and our "turn the other cheek" mentality add to the support structure of our divisive leadership hierarchy. Also of influence are examples set by those who uphold the standards of American leadership and its implementation. They instill within the minds of our youth, the diverse ways of achievement and social ascension.

An important factor to consider is that leadership is essential not only at the higher levels of our society but more so within the early development of our youth, in places such as the home, community and family environments. This early development is essential to instilling a moral compass within our youth, providing them with the necessary characteristics essential to creating a productive social and inner developmental leadership structure.

If greed, abandonment, irresponsibility, absence of the inner strength to excel, and the pursuit of loophole idealism shape the minds and consciousness of our youth at the earliest of age, we are in effect creating and maintaining the very generation that the adult population has viewed with disgust and despair.

From Pre-School to the Penitentiary:
A Candid Examination of a Vicious Cycle

It should be our charge to influence leadership at the highest levels of our society. It is our greater responsibility to influence within ourselves the consciousness of our own levels and leading examples of social and moral justice.

Accountability

Those who would profess to be architects and agents of empowerment and positive development within any culture must be vigilant, sincere and ultimately accountable for their actions. Likewise, those who would do nothing, who would criticize and perpetuate the cycles of negativity and counterproduction, should and must be held accountable as well.

The engrained thought processes of fear and self-depravation etched into the innate thought processes of black people have left indelible scars upon the psyche that adversely affect our ability to visualize the productive powers of independent thought and progression.

Independent thought and pursuit of holistic progress can lead to belief in accountability—recognition that one's words and actions align with an overall sense of ethical, moral and spiritual connection within oneself and between other people. An inner compass, developed over time and in concert with adult guidance, directs a person's decisions and behavior—the accountable person embraces other people's review and assessment and is willing to "open the books" and participate in an inventory.

Outreach: Intangibles

However, when we as a culture give in to our history of enslavement we concede a fundamental tendency to be negotiable with our loyalties, while lowering our productive standards and curtailing our ascension. We are in a sense perpetuating a culture of our own demise which opposes accountability. This intangible is an important element of youths' development.

The accountability of black people in America is skewed beyond normal perception. Our dilemma is quite unique as many black people in America question the levels of their accountability and what it may encompass. For us, this intangible is multi-layered, sometimes subtle and vital to how young people discover how they define "success."

For example, as black people seek the mobility to transcend the often adversarial conditions of American society, we ponder our commitment to those who have been omitted from the equation of the American Dream. Our unification during the eras of Slavery, the Jim Crow era and the Civil Rights Movement has created an everlasting moral and spiritual relationship within our culture. But some of us wonder whether we can sufficiently "give back" some of our success to those less fortunate while also maintaining the drive and ambition that might sustain our improved status. Or we find ourselves struggling not to "blame the victim" as we realize this would erode our thought processes toward the less fortunate. Will these kinds of tendencies cause failure with accountability, some of us wonder. We question our accountability (if any) in support of those who exist within the social injustices of American culture.

On the other hand, as black people we firmly believe we are citizens of the United States but there is an instinctive part of us that continues to feel somewhat detached from the whole of American society. A conflicting and rebellious nature, in defiance of the "status quo" can divide our commitment to embrace the trustworthiness of the American cultural reality.

We have fought many battles throughout American history, many in support of this nation and many in spite of this nation. The Revolutionary War, the Civil War, World Wars One and Two, Vietnam, and countless other conflicts around the world are among those in which we have participated alongside fellow combatants. Generally speaking, black people in America, despite the realities concerning the social and moral injustices of our society, have demonstrated extreme acts of accountability and loyalty in service of this nation.

What remains perplexing in relation to the accountability of black people in America lies within individual and/or personal standards of accountability.

While many black people in America have transcended the unbalanced levels of their condition, many have created a perpetual legacy of an inability to thrive which has become generational in its effect. The cultural conditions of gang violence, black-on-black genocide, illegitimacy of our children, and our lack of a productive power base within our communities, are elements relevant to our overall discontent and willingness to distance ourselves from being held accountable for these and other adversities.

The systematic processes of the educational arena, poor health care, self-destructive living conditions, and the criminal justice system drastically influence and contribute to the continuation of this vicious cycle of counterproduction and cultural stagnation.

To counteract these erosive conditions from both a systematic and cultural perspective, black people in America must rediscover their identity. We must renew our commitment to accountability.

We have compromised the strength of our spirituality for a facade of our current religious order. We have bought into the "bootstrap" ideology of a crippling societal hierarchy. We have abandoned the element of struggle within an unjust sociological system. This struggle is endemic to the need to readjust our individual and cultural compasses as we rediscover our ethics, morality, "teachable moments" of learning from mistakes, and otherwise identify who we are—the good, the bad, the ups and the downs.

Anger often exists within the essence of accountability. At times it is necessary to rebel and become somewhat disobedient in order to correct the course of misdirection.

As black people in America, accountability is fundamental to the source of our aspiration and essential to the discovery of our own sincerity.

What would become of our culture and our legacy if we would choose to abandon our responsibilities of self and instead, carry the mantel of selective history and walk within the shadow of an inferior destination? Equally important, where will our youth be and who will they become unless we embrace our and their accountability?

Summary

Within the most common mind-set of an individual exists a desire to postpone, or to set defensive parameters in the wake of obtaining information that tends to disrupt or unbalance the familiar flow of everyday life.

To be made aware of a medical condition, the death of a loved one, an eviction notice, or the loss of a job are among the many realities that most of us, if given the choice, would rather not to confront. However, these circumstances, traumatic in their unveiling serve as an ironic creation of our catalyst to begin the process of realization. This process can inspire us to confront and engage the obstacles of adversity defiantly standing before us.

It is a logical assumption to state that to combat and conquer any traumatic or dire condition, one must first examine the symptomatic elements of the condition as well as its current and potential levels of severity.

In a sociological and developmental sense these conditions exist within the basic, structural design of American society that profoundly impacts the mobility of the black, brown and poor segments of our society. As we do so often within our personal lives, for many years we have chosen to postpone dealing with them or we set defensive parameters, ultimately becoming an interactive participant and character of the condition itself.

In this particular scope of work I have elected to focus on the intangible as well as the more tangible cornerstones of our foundation whose priority involves stopping the vicious cycle driving our youth from preschool to the penitentiary. We must

Summary

create a structural design that is developmentally constructive in its reality.

Throughout this book, I have spoken of missteps and accomplishments, of hypocrisy and of sincerity, of cultural self-destruction and cultural renewal, of not realizing one's greatness and of the acknowledgment of greatness, and of spiritual and psychological submission and its conquering.

I have also spoken of the importance of pursuing a re-bonding of the black male and female to establish stronger relationships and to develop greater mutual respect for each other. This is important not just for adults but for our youths' development as well. Our youth need more of an embrace and a stronger support structure from the adult population. Our tendency to mute our voices must change; we must become vocal advocates of the existence and reestablishment of a cohesive family structure which is essential to our future development. We need to demonstrate the responsibility of the family to provide a solid moral compass for our youth. We also must show them that it may be necessary to become socially disobedient to correct the courses of misdirection, but the disobedience needs to serve the greater good—the ability to participate openly and honestly in accountability.

To seek solutions to transcend the social, environmental and psychological elements of counterproduction that exist within the developmental consciousness and mind-set of our culture means we must acknowledge the diabolical, innate implants within our spiritual and moral psyche. We must examine how we live with a complex of inferiority conditionally instilling within us a complex of inferiority that subconsciously manipulates our thought processes of desire and determination.

From Pre-School to the Penitentiary:
A Candid Examination of a Vicious Cycle

While it is primarily essential to look within ourselves to access the elements of our own uniqueness and greatness to conquer the obstacles before us, it is also vital that we look deeply into the consciousness of an oppressive hierarchy that was in the process of designing our demise long before we encountered them.

If this book serves to move you to constructive anger to act positively upon what you have read, especially when dealing with our youth, you have proven that the pathways of our solutions are indeed perpetual.

Appendix

Criminal Justice/Injustice

Juvenile Arrest and Incarceration:

- Black children were more than twice as likely as white children to be arrested. From ages 10-17 a black youth was more than five times as likely as a white youth to be arrested for a violent crime.

- Black children constituted 15.1 percent of the overall population.

  They constituted:

- Thirty-one percent of all juvenile arrests.

- Twenty-five percent of all juvenile arrests for drug abuse violations.

- Fifty-one percent of all juvenile arrests for violent offenses.

- In *Miller v. Alabama* (June 25, 2012), the U.S. Supreme Court ruled that juveniles could not be subject to mandatory life sentences without the possibility of parole. Of the approximately 2,500 juveniles across the nation serving life sentences, the Supreme Court decision could change the sentences of more than 2,000 of them. A study found that 56 percent of juveniles serving life sentences without parole were black. In 17 states, more than 60 percent of juveniles serving life sentences without parole were black. For example:

- In Alabama, it was 84 percent (75 of 89).

- In Maryland, 79 percent (15 of 19).

- In South Carolina, 79 percent (11 of 14).

Sources:

Ashley Nellis, "The Lives of Juvenile Lifers: Findings from a National Survey," Washington, DC: The Sentencing Project. sentencing project.org/.../jj_The_Lives_of_Juvenile_Lifers.pdf

"Criminal Justice Fact Sheet," NAACP. www.naacp.org/pages/criminal-justice-fact-sheet

"Facts and Infographics about Life without Parole for Children," Washington, DC: The Campaign for the Fair Sentencing of Youth. Fairsentencingofyouth.org/what-is-jlwop/

Appendix

"Juvenile Justice, Basic Statistics," Frontline PBS. www.pbs.org/wgbh/pages/frontline/shows/juvenile/stats/basic.html

No Place for Kids: The Case for Reducing Juvenile Incarceration, Annie E. Casey Foundation, October 4, 2011. www.aecf.org/resources/no-place-for-kids-full-report/

Adult Incarceration:

- Black males are more than five times as likely as white males to be incarcerated some time in their lifetime. This group is even larger for females, with black females born in 2001 more than six times as likely as their white peers to be incarcerated at some point.

- One in 12 working-age black men was in prison or jail compared to one in 57 working-age white men.

- One in 10 black men ages 30 through 34 were held in state or federal prison or jail compared to one in 61 white men that same age.

- Black adult men were incarcerated in state and federal facilities at over six times the rate of white adult men and black adult women were incarcerated at more than two-and-a-half times the rate of white adult women.

Sources:

Adam Liptak, "1 in 100 U.S. Adults Behind Bars, New Study Says," *New York Times,* February 28, 2008. www.nytimes.com/2008/02/28/us/28cnd-prison.html

"Criminal Justice Fact Sheet," NAACP. www.naacp.org/pages/criminal-justice-fact-sheet

U.S. Department of Justice, "Prisoners in 2013," Bureau of Justice Statistics. www.bjs.gov/content/pub/pdf/p13.pdf

Global Comparisons of U.S. Incarceration:

- The U.S. has five percent of the world's population, but 25 percent of the world's prison inmate population.

- In 2008, 2.3 million or one in 100 adults in America were behind bars.

Appendix

- The rate of incarceration in the U.S. climbed from 221 to 743 per 100,000 from 1980 to 2009. This is more than a 300 percent increase.

- The U.S. houses more inmates than all European nations combined.

Sources:

Adam Liptak, "U.S. Prison Population Dwarfs that of Other Nations," *New York Times,* April 23, 2008. www.nytimes.com/2008/04/23/world/americas/23iht-23prison.12253738.html?

"International Incarceration Comparisons," Prison Policy Initiative. www.prisonpolicy.org/global/

The Educational System

- Only seven percent of public school teachers are black and only two percent are black males.

- Black children were 16 percent of sixth through eighth graders but 42 percent of students in those grades who were held back a year.

From Pre-School to the Penitentiary:
A Candid Examination of a Vicious Cycle

- Although black students comprised only 18 percent of students in public schools they represented:

- Forty percent of all students who experienced corporal punishment;

- Thirty-five percent of all students who received one out-of-school suspension;

- Forty-six percent of all students who received multiple out-of-school suspensions;

- Thirty-nine percent of all students expelled.

- At age four, black children scored significantly behind white children in their proficiency in letter, number and shape recognition.

- Black students score the lowest of any racial/ethnic student group on the ACT and SAT college entrance exams.

Appendix

- Thirty–five percent of the nation's black students attended one of 1,700 "dropout factories," high schools where less than 60 percent of the freshman class graduate in four years; only eight percent of the nation's white students attended such schools.

- Black males age 18 and over represented only five percent of the total college student population, but 36 percent of the total prison population.

Sources:

"African Americans and Education," NAACP. https://www.naacp.org/page/-/education%20documents/AfricanAmericansAndEducation.pdf

"Are We Closing the School Discipline Gap? New Research Identifies Districts with Worst Suspension Records," Los Angeles: The Civil Rights Project. http://civilrightsproject.ucla.edu/news/press-releases

"Dropout Factories," Associated Press. http://hosted.ap.org/specials/interactives/wdc/dropout/index.html?SITE=AP

From Pre-School to the Penitentiary:
A Candid Examination of a Vicious Cycle

Jesse Holland, "Studies Highlight Teacher-Student 'Diversity Gap,'" *Boston Globe,* May 5, 2014. https://www.bostonglobe.com/news/nation/2014

Lindsey Cook, "U.S. Education: Still Separate and Unequal," *U.S. News & World Report,* January 28, 2015. http://www.usnews.com/news/blogs/data-mine/2015/01/28/us-education-still-separate-and-unequal

"Racial/Ethnic Enrollment in Public Schools," National Center for Education Statistics. www/nces.ed.gov/programs/coe/indicator_cge.asp

"The Test Score Gap: Secrets of the SAT," Frontline PBS. www.pbs.org/wgbh/pages/frontline/shows/sats/etc/gap.html

U.S. Department of Education, "Data Snapshot: School Discipline – Civil Rights Data Collection," Office for Civil Rights, Issue Brief No. 1, March 2014. http://ocrdata.ed.gov/Downloads/CRDC-School-Discipline-Snapshot.pdf

U.S. Department of Education, "Fast Facts: Public and Private School Comparisons," National Center for Education Statistics, 2013. https://nces.ed.gov/fastfacts/display.asp?id=55

Appendix

The Community

War Zones of Violence:

Family violence, gun violence and community violence threaten children's sense of security, hope and vision for the future.

- Black children have the highest rate of abuse and neglect. Black children comprise 28.1 percent of deaths from child mistreatment.

- More than one in five victims of child abuse and neglect were black.

- Over 90 percent of firearm deaths of black children and teens were homicides (1,092) and six percent were suicides; among white children and teens just under half of all firearm deaths in 209 were homicides (730) and 46 percent were suicides.

- While the annual number of firearm deaths of white children and teens decreased by 44 percent, the deaths of black children and teens increased by 30 percent.

From Pre-School to the Penitentiary:
A Candid Examination of a Vicious Cycle

- Forty-three percent of all children and youth killed by firearms were black. Black males ages 15 to 19 were more than eight times as likely as white males and more than two-and-a-half times as Hispanic males in the same age group to be killed in a firearm homicide.

- The number of black children and teens killed by gunfire is nearly 13 times the number of black men.

Sources:

"Child Abuse and Neglect Statistics," American Humane Association. www.americanhumane.org/children/stop-child-abuse-and-neglect-statistics.html

Janell Ross, "Gun Violence's No. 1 Target: Black Children," The Root, October 7, 2013. http://www.theroot.com/articles/culture/2013/10/gun_violence_leading_killer_of_black_children_why_we_need_to_care_about_the_gun_debate.html

U.S. Department of Health and Human Services, "Fourth National Incidence Study of Child Abuse and Neglect," Administration for Children and Families, January 2010. www.acf.hhs.gov/sites/default/files/opre/nis4_report_exec_summ_pdf_jan2010.pdf

Appendix

Family Structure and History

Family Structure:

Poverty can fray family bonds. Children are left without family support and often face daunting challenges.

- Fifty-one percent of black children live with only their mother. Black children are more than three times as likely to live with their mother only as are white children.

- Black children are more than two-and-a-half times as likely as white children to live with neither parent. Almost five percent of black children live with grandparents, and just under two percent of black children live with other relatives.

- Black children are more than twice as likely as white children to be in foster care.

- Black children are over six times as likely as white children to have a parent in prison.

- Black babies were more than twice as likely as white babies to be born to a teen mother in 2012.

From Pre-School to the Penitentiary:
A Candid Examination of a Vicious Cycle

Sources:

Child Trends Data Bank compiles data on trends related to children and families on a variety of topics, drawing from U.S. Census Bureau statistics and other sources. Search by topic (e.g., foster care, number of parents in households, etc.) at http://www.child trends.org/databank/indicators-by-topic-area/

Michael and Michelle Anthony, eds., *A Theology of Family Ministry,* Nashville: B&H Publishing Group, 2011.

The American Dream

Poverty destroys childhood and can destroy children. More than one in five children in the U.S.—16.1 million children—live at or below the poverty line.

- Black children are over three times as likely to be poor (38.8 percent) as white children (12.5) percent.

- Black children are over three times as likely as white children to live in extreme poverty. Extreme poverty is defined as half of the poverty level or less ($11,511 for a family of four).

Appendix

- The 4.3 million black children living in poverty represented an increase of 675,000 poor children.

- Black children under five are the poorest group of children after young Native American children. Over 42 percent of young black children are poor compared to 15.0 percent of young white children. Young black children are three-and-a-half times as likely as white children to live in extreme poverty.

- Sixty-six percent of black children were raised in neighborhoods with a poverty rate of at least 20 percent, compared to only six percent of white children.

- Black babies are more than twice as likely to die before their first birthday as white babies.

Sources:

"Poverty in the United States: A Snapshot," New York: National Center for Law and Economic Justice. www.nclej.org/poverty-in-the-us.php

The State of Black Children in America, Children's Defense Fund, March 28, 2014.www.childrensdefensefund.org/library/ data/

From Pre-School to the Penitentiary:
A Candid Examination of a Vicious Cycle

state-of-black-children-2014.pdf?utm_source=2014-SOAC-
AdRes&utm_medium=link&utm_campaign=2014-SOAC

Job Status and Income of Young Adults:

The recession has created an extremely difficult labor market for all youth, but minority youth face the harshest impact. Black college graduates compared to other graduates, for example, have the highest unemployment rate and the highest levels of education loan debt. These facts bode ill for black wealth creation.

- An average of nearly half of black high school graduates ages 17 to 20 were unemployed—the highest unemployment rate of any racial/ethnic group.

- The unemployment rate for black males age 20 and over (13.5 percent) was more than twice as high as the unemployment rate for white males (6.2 percent).

- Black males ages 25 to 64 are more likely to have a lower income than white males with similar educational backgrounds. The gap in median earnings between black and white males with some high school education but no diploma was approximately $9,700. The gap between black and white males with master's degrees was approximately 23,500.

Appendix

- The typical black household had a net worth (assets minus debts) of $5,677 compared to $113,149 for white households. Black households were more than twice as likely as white households to have zero or negative net worth, with over a third of black households in this situation.

Sources:

Drew Desilver, "Black Unemployment Is Consistently Twice that of Whites," Washington, DC: Pew Research Center, August 21, 2013. http://www.pewresearch.org/fact-tank/2013/ 08/21/ through-good-times-and-bad-black-unemployment-is-consistently-double-that-of-whites/

Reniqua Allen, "For Black Men, a Permanent Recession," Al Jazeera America, October 9, 2014. http://america.aljazeera.com/ features/ 2014/10/for-black-men-a-permanent-recession.html

"Why Is the Black Unemployment Rate So High?" *The Atlantic,* June 12, 2014. http://www.theatlantic.com/business/ archive/ 2014/06/why-is-the-black-unemployment-rate-so-high/372667/

From Pre-School to the Penitentiary:
A Candid Examination of a Vicious Cycle

About the Author

I am originally from Buffalo, New York; but have spent most of my life in Louisville, Ky.

A son of deceased parents I am the youngest of three brothers.

A graduate of Central High School in Louisville and an Honorably Discharged Veteran of the U.S. Army I spent two years in college, with an interest in sociology.

Growing up with an innate nature of rebellion, I paid a heavy price in my earlier adult years because of my stubborn and somewhat counter culture idealism.

This nature of rebellion served as my catalyst to seek out and to develop a more articulate level of self expression.

My father, an accomplished writer and poet and my mother, serving as my spiritual cornerstone inspired me to embark upon my own journey of creativity.

I began to write poetry and was soon speaking and reading at organizations and universities in the Louisville area. I was also travelling as far as San Diego and Los Angeles California to perform and speak in various areas. My poetry garnered me various awards and I negotiated performance contracts to do motivational outreaches in the public school system and in various so-called higher risk neighborhoods in the Louisville area. It was soon after that I had written and published the first of three books and created The Awareness Project. They are as follows: "Perpetual

Appendix

Domain" Dog House Publishing 1994, "Inner Strength Defies the Skeptic" Immediex Publishing 2006, and my latest, "From Pre School to the Penitentiary" African American Images Publishing 2015.

My work experiences include; Street Gang outreach and intervention, working with 'Behavior Disordered" students in the alternative and public school system and Program Design and implementation relating to community development and mobilization.

I currently work with youth and families in search of personal and social development. I continue to utilize The Awareness Project in designing and implementing a vast array of developmental outreach strategies.

To Request Services:

Contact: Duane Campbell (The Awareness Project)

P.O. Box 1262

Louisville, KY. 40201

E-MAIL: iamtheglow@hotmail.com

Phone: 502-418-0211

Endnotes

[1] James Weldon Johnson and John Rosamond Johnson, "Lift Ev'ry Voice and Sing" (also called "The Black National Anthem"), 1899.

[2] Martin Luther King, Jr., "Out of the Long Night," *The Gospel Messenger,*
February 8, 1958.

[3] For more details about this disproportion see the Criminal Justice/Injustice portion of this book 's Appendix.

[4] See the American Dream portion of this book's Appendix for further details.

[5] The use of "church" is meant to include all Christian denominations.

[6] Fred Barbash, "Charleston's Emanuel AME Church: A Legacy of Heroes and Martyrs," *Washington Post,* June 26, 2015. http://www.washington post.com/news/morning-mix/wp/2015/06/26/the-turbulent-birth-of-the-emanuel-ame-church-and-why-it-terrified-white-charleston.

[7] "(1868) Rev. Henry McNeal Turner, 'I Claim the Rights of a Man, '" Black Past. http://www.blackpast.org/1868-reverend-henry-mcneal-turner-i-claim-rights-man.

Endnotes

[8] Dennis C. Dickerson, "Our History," African Methodist Episcopal Church Official Website. http://www.ame-church.com/our-church/our-history.

[9] Duane Campbell, "The Psychology of Oppression," *Inner Strength Defies the Skeptic* (Immediex, 2006).

[10] See the Appendix of this book for further details.